Manufactured by Amazon.ca
Bolton, ON

27249996R00061